DINOSAUR HUNTERS

By Kate McMullan

Illustrated by John R. Jones

Random House New York

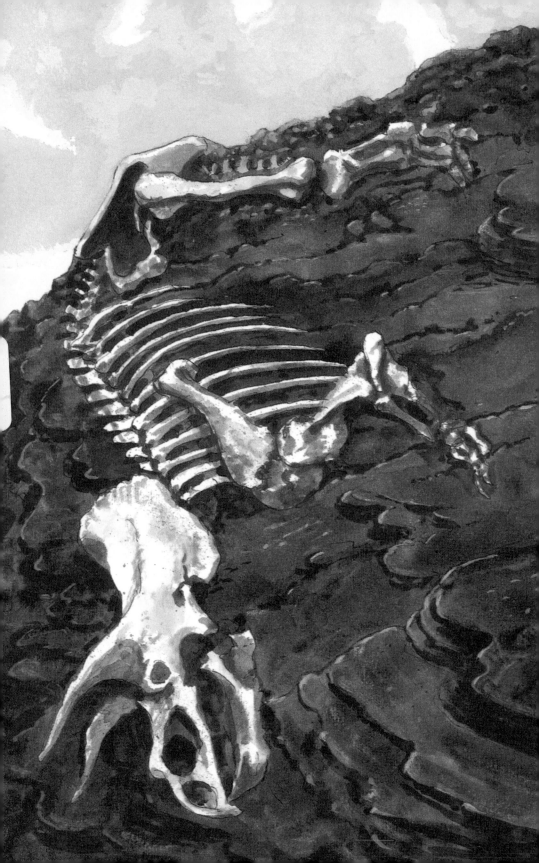

1

Secrets in Stone

Jim Jensen was a famous dinosaur hunter. He discovered a meat-eater that no one had ever seen before. He also found a giant dinosaur. He called it *Supersaurus* (SOO-pur-SAW-rus), or "super lizard." Jim Jensen was one of the best dinosaur hunters of his time. That's how he got the nickname "Dinosaur Jim."

Of course dinosaurs don't live on earth today. The last ones disappeared about 65 million years ago. So how could Dinosaur Jim hunt dinosaurs if there weren't any around?

To find out, imagine the earth 150 million years ago. Many seas are warm and shallow. The ground is covered with mosses and ferns. There are many tall trees with fan-shaped leaves. Dinosaurs of all shapes and sizes roam the earth.

Some of the dinosaurs are the size of a chicken. Other dinosaurs are as tall as a four-story building. Some have scales and tail spikes. Some have feathers. There are no people yet. It is the middle of the Mesozoic (MES-uh-ZO-ick) Era. It is the Age of Dinosaurs.

Picture a gigantic *Apatosaurus* (ah-PAT-uh-SAW-rus) walking on a riverbank. This *Apatosaurus* is old and weak. It bends its long neck and takes one last drink from the river. Then it falls on its side in the mud. It is dead.

Most of the soft flesh of the *Apatosaurus* is quickly eaten by animals. The rest rots away. In time, the hard bones sink into the mud. The mud protects the bones. They do not rot away.

For millions of years, the bones lie under the ground. Rain falls. It seeps down through the ground, dissolving minerals in the rocks. The rainwater carries these minerals along as it trickles down to the bones.

Like all bones, the *Apatosaurus* bones are filled with tiny holes. The rainwater seeps into these holes. The water evaporates. But the minerals in the water stay and harden in the bones. Little by little, what once was bone turns to stone. The bones of the *Apatosaurus* are now stone. They are fossils.

Water deposits minerals in the bone.

The bone turns into a stone fossil.

Many things may have happened to these fossil bones. Earthquakes may have rattled them. Volcanoes may have erupted and buried them under lava. Glaciers may have dragged tons of ice over them. Oceans may have flowed over the land and covered the bones with layers of sand and broken shells. The weight of the lava or ice or sand presses on the mud around the bones. Slowly the mud turns to stone.

Millions of years pass. The land shifts. Mountains rise. The *Apatosaurus* bones are pushed up. A few stick out from the edge of a high cliff. Sunlight is shining on the *Apatosaurus* bones once again.

It is fossilized bones like these ones that Dinosaur Jim hunted. Like other dinosaur hunters, he was a paleontologist (PAY-lee-on-TOL-uh-jist), a scientist who studies plants and animals from the distant past.

What secrets can dinosaur fossils tell pale-ontologists? Can they tell them what a dinosaur looked like? How fast it ran? What it ate? Paleontologists want to find out all they can about the world of dinosaurs. And fossils—and the rocks they are buried in—are their best clues.

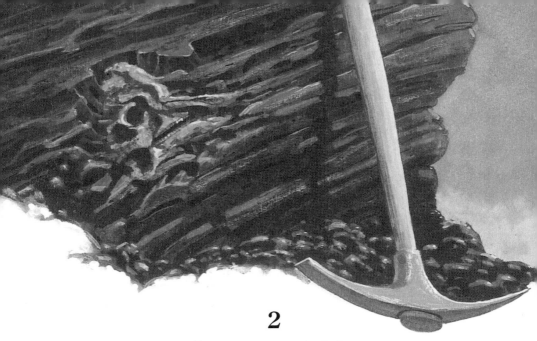

2
The Giant Tooth Mystery

People have been finding dinosaur fossils for thousands of years. They have found them in cliffs and beside lakes. They have found them while digging for coal. The word *fossil* comes from Latin. It means "dug up." And that is usually how people find them!

Until about two hundred years ago, people who found huge fossils did not know what they were. That's because they didn't know dinosaurs had ever existed. Some thought the big bones came from large animals that they had seen or read about, such as hippos or elephants. But they never knew that very different creatures from the animals they were aware of had once lived on earth.

But some of the bones people found were *huge*. They were too big to have come from even the biggest hippo or elephant. These enormous bones led some people to believe in giants and ogres. Some Native Americans thought the big bones were from skeletons of giant serpents.

In China, the big bones were said to come from powerful dragons. People ground these "dragon bones" into powder. They mixed the bone powder into a potion and drank it. They believed drinking dragon bones would make them powerful, too.

About four hundred years ago, a man named Bernard Palissy had another idea. He was a famous French pottery maker. When he went to a riverbank to collect clay to make his pots, he found many tiny fossils in the clay. He studied the fossils and wrote that they were the remains of living creatures. This was not a new idea. But Palissy wrote something else as well. He wrote that some of these creatures no longer lived on earth. They had completely disappeared. They were *extinct*.

Did Palissy become famous for his discovery? No! People were frightened by his ideas. And Palissy was put in prison.

As time went by, some people became more open to new ideas about how the world might have been thousands or even millions of years ago. But others did not want to think that the world could change so much.

Then, in the 1820s, a huge fossil tooth was found in England. No one knows exactly how it was found. One legend says that a fossil collector named Mary Ann Mantell went for a walk while her husband, Gideon, a country doctor, was with a patient. The road was being repaired. In some broken-up rocks, Mary Ann saw what looked like a huge stone tooth.

Mary Ann knew the big tooth was a fossil. She picked it up. Later, she showed it to Gideon, who was a fossil expert.

Gideon knew the tooth had belonged to a plant-eater because it was flat and had ridges. It was worn down from chewing food. It was almost as big as the tooth of an elephant. But it looked nothing like an elephant's tooth.

Gideon knew a lot about rocks. He could tell from the rock around the tooth that this fossil was very old. It was from the Mesozoic Era. He knew what kinds of fossils had been found in rock that old—reptile fossils.

Gideon was puzzled. No reptile that he knew about chewed its food. Reptiles gulped their food, so their teeth didn't become worn down. The big tooth was a mystery.

Could the tooth have belonged to a giant, plant-eating reptile? A type of reptile that no longer lived on earth?

Gideon spent years looking in nearby rock quarries for more fossils. At last he found some big fossil bones.

Gideon Mantell took the tooth and bones to a museum in London. He showed the tooth to other scientists. One famous scientist said it was a rhinoceros tooth. No one agreed with Gideon that it might be the tooth of a gigantic reptile.

Gideon tried to find something that looked like the giant tooth. For a long time, he found nothing. Then one day he met a scientist who was studying iguanas. An iguana is a large lizard found in Central and South America. It can grow to be more than five feet long. Gideon showed him the big fossil tooth. The scientist showed him an iguana tooth. At last! Here was the tooth of a living reptile that looked like the mystery tooth. Only the fossil tooth was much, much bigger.

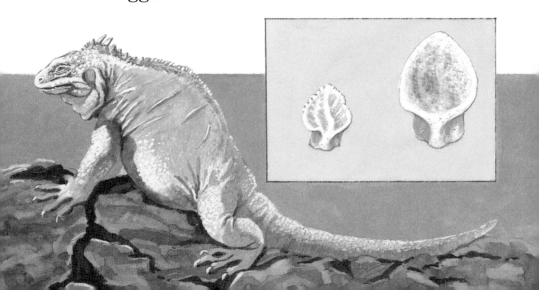

Now Gideon believed the fossil tooth had belonged to an animal that looked like an iguana. Only it wasn't five feet long. Gideon believed it was a hundred feet long! He named his creature *Iguanodon* (ih-GWON-uh-don). That means "iguana tooth."

Gideon did not have a whole *Iguanodon* skeleton. But from the bones he had, he tried to figure out what an *Iguanodon* might have looked like. He thought the bones showed that the creature had walked on all four legs. He thought a pointed bone was a horn. He drew an *Iguanodon* with a horn on its nose.

Years later, several complete *Iguanodon* skeletons were found. They were only about thirty feet long. The bones showed that *Iguanodon* walked on its hind legs some of the time. And the horn on its nose was really a spike on *Iguanodon*'s "thumb"!

The top picture shows what Gideon thought an *Iguanodon* looked like. The bottom picture shows what an *Iguanodon* really looked like.

Gideon Mantell made some mistakes. But he had made an important discovery, too. He wrote a paper on *Iguanodon*. He was one of the first people to say that long ago, before there were any humans, giant reptiles lived on earth. And then they became extinct.

Two hundred years before, Bernard Palissy had been thrown into prison for saying nearly the same thing. But Gideon Mantell became famous. Now the world couldn't wait to find out more about these enormous reptiles.

Soon the fossils of other extinct reptiles were discovered. They showed that in some ways, these creatures were like modern reptiles. But in other ways, they were very different. For one thing, the legs of modern reptiles, such as crocodiles and lizards, stick out from the sides of their bodies. They slither and crawl, with their bellies low to the ground. But the big fossil bones showed that most extinct reptiles stood with their feet directly *under* their bodies. They would have walked upright, like an elephant.

In 1842, a scientist named Richard Owen decided that these extinct reptiles needed a name of their own. He called them *Dinosauria*. In Greek, *deinos* means "fearfully great" and *sauros* means "lizard." Today we call them dinosaurs.

3
Here Come
the Dinosaur Hunters!

English dinosaur hunters discovered many new kinds of dinosaurs. Their discoveries made newspaper headlines. People wanted to know everything about these extinct giants.

Artists painted pictures of what they thought dinosaurs looked like. Sculptors built life-size dinosaur statues.

For New Year's Eve in 1853, a scientist sent party invitations to other scientists. When the guests showed up, they found a table set for twenty-two people *inside* the body cavity of an almost-finished statue of an *Iguanodon*!

Word of the giant fossil bones spread quickly. By the 1850s, dinosaur fever had hit America, too. At this time, new railroad beds were being dug out west. Prospectors were digging for gold in California and Colorado. With all that digging going on, fossils were uncovered nearly every day. The western United States was a dinosaur hunter's dream.

Like cowboys, early dinosaur hunters in America were rugged. They loved adventure. They carried chisels and rock hammers. They also carried rifles and bowie knives. The West was a wild and dangerous place.

Dinosaur hunters often lived off the land. They shot their food each day. They had to know where to find water in the desert. They drove stubborn pack mules and clumsy wagons.

Dinosaur hunters called the place they worked a "dig." They had to figure out how to get huge bones out of solid rock with just picks, shovels, and ropes. When they dug up the bones, dinosaur hunters sometimes wrapped them in cloth or in flour sacks. They put the bones in their wagons or packed them onto the backs of their mules. Then they headed for the nearest railroad. They shipped the bones back east to fossil collectors and museums.

Two of the most famous bone collectors were Dr. Edward Cope and Dr. Othniel Marsh. These two paleontologists started out as friends. But soon they became enemies. Each one wanted *all* the dinosaur bones for himself!

Both Cope and Marsh found lots of bones. Each one wanted to be the first to show off his dinosaur skeletons. When Cope found the bones of an *Elasmosaurus* (ih-LAS-muh-SAW-rus), he was in such a hurry to show off the skeleton that he put the head on the tail end! Marsh made sure that everyone knew about Cope's big mistake. But later, he made one of his own. He put the skull of another dinosaur on top of an *Apatosaurus* skeleton. He called this "new" dinosaur *Brontosaurus* (BRON-tuh-SAW-rus). His mistake was not corrected for almost one hundred years!

In the 1870s, railroad workers began finding big bones at Como Bluff, Wyoming. The place was so loaded with fossils that one trapper built himself a cabin out of dinosaur bones!

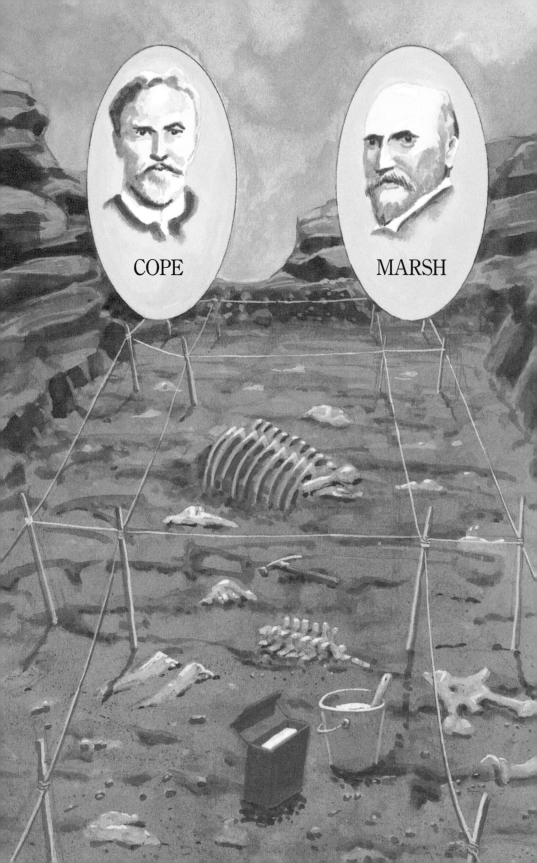

COPE

MARSH

Cope and Marsh heard about all these bones. Both men headed west and set up digs. Cope accused Marsh of stealing fossils from his dig. Marsh accused Cope of the same thing. But Marsh wanted to make sure that Cope did not get any of his fossils. So he had his workers set up dynamite—and he blew up his own dig!

Other scientists were ashamed of the way Cope and Marsh fought. They thought it gave paleontologists a bad name. But they had to admit one thing. The "bone war" led to the discovery of tons and tons of dinosaur bones!

Marsh and his team of dinosaur hunters were the first to find *Apatosaurus, Stegosaurus* (STEG-uh-SAW-rus), and *Triceratops* (try-SAIR-uh-tops). If you visit Yale University's Peabody Museum, you can see Marsh's dinosaurs. You can see many of Cope's dinosaurs at the American Museum of Natural History, in New York City.

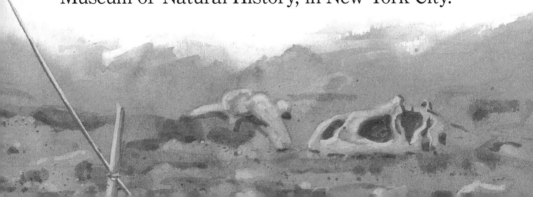

4

Hunting Giants

Unlike fossil hunters a hundred years ago, today's dinosaur hunters have modern tools. They drive trucks instead of pack mules and wagons. Sometimes computers can help them discover where big bones are buried. But the thrill of finding dinosaur bones hasn't changed. And neither has the long, hard work.

When dinosaur hunters find a place to dig, they make camp. In hot places, they may build a wooden roof over the spot where they will dig. The roof protects the fossils that are exposed during digging. It shades the dinosaur hunters, too.

On some digs, dinosaur hunters use a back-hoe to remove layers of rock and dirt above the fossils. Once they get close to a bone, they switch to handheld tools such as chisels, awls, and hammers. Sometimes they even use dental picks! Dinosaur hunters have to be careful. One wrong move can shatter a huge dinosaur bone.

Sometimes dinosaur hunters will dig out a big chunk of rock with fossilized bones in it. They do not chip away the rock around the bones. Instead, the rock is left around the fossils to help protect them. The entire rock is wrapped in paper towels and covered with plaster. Then it is put in a crate and sent to a museum.

Other times, bones are taken out of the rock right at a dig. But dinosaur hunters don't hurry. They take pictures of the bones just as they are in the ground. Sometimes they make drawings, too. Then each bone is numbered. All this work will help later, when a skeleton is put together again in a museum laboratory.

Next, dinosaur hunters pour a type of glue on each bone as it lies cradled in the rock. The glue hardens the bones. When the glue is dry, the bone can usually be taken safely out of the rock.

Little bones can be wrapped in foil and packed in boxes. But bigger bones need more protection. First, they are covered with a thin wrapping, like tissue paper, paper towels, or foil. Then burlap strips are soaked in wet plaster.

These strips are wrapped around the bones.
The wrapping keeps the plaster from sticking
to the bones. The plaster dries into a hard cast,
like the kind doctors make for broken bones.
These casts, or jackets, protect big bones while
they are being shipped.

Really big dinosaur bones can be really big problems for dinosaur hunters. If large trucks can get close to a dig, dinosaur hunters can use powerful winches to lift the bones out of the ground. This makes it possible for today's dinosaur hunters to collect bigger dinosaur bones than ever before. And for many years, when it came to hunting BIG dinosaurs, nobody beat Dinosaur Jim.

Dinosaur hunters like Dinosaur Jim find fossils in all sorts of ways. Sometimes people call them up with tips. An oil field worker might report that she's seen some big bones buried in the sand. A quarry digger might tell them he's uncovered a giant skull. A miner might phone to say that while he was digging for coal, he found a huge backbone. And if a call comes? A dinosaur hunter is on the way!

Dinosaur Jim hunted giant dinosaurs outside. He hunted them inside museums, too. Once, while poking around a storeroom, Dinosaur Jim discovered a huge arm bone. It was the biggest one he'd ever seen. A tag said that the bone had been found in Colorado. Were

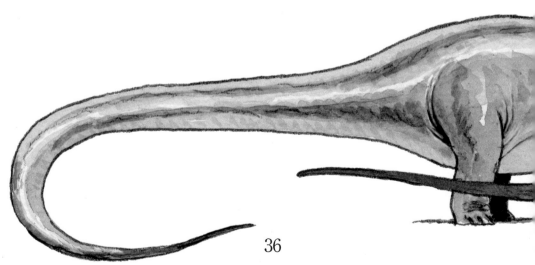

more of this big dinosaur's bones buried in the same place? Dinosaur Jim headed to Colorado to find out.

Dinosaur Jim started digging. His hunch was right! He and his crew dug up part of a skeleton of the largest dinosaur ever found!

Until Dinosaur Jim's discovery, the forty-foot-tall *Brachiosaurus* (BRACK-ee-uh-SAW-rus) was the biggest known dinosaur. But Dinosaur Jim's new dinosaur was even bigger. It would have been 120 feet long! That's why he called it *Supersaurus*.

But Dinosaur Jim's discovery wasn't the biggest dinosaur. In 1991, hikers in New Mexico found an even *bigger* dinosaur. They saw a long line of huge white rocks poking out of the earth. The rocks turned out to be the bones of a huge dinosaur's tail. The hikers called a dinosaur hunter, Dr. David Gillette. He named this new dinosaur *Seismosaurus* (SIZE-muh-SAW-rus), or "earthshaking lizard."

Then, in 1993, a sheep rancher in Argentina saw what looked like a log made of stone. Two South American dinosaur hunters came to check it out. The log turned out to be a bone of an even bigger dinosaur. They named it *Argentinosaurus* (AR-jun-TEE-nuh-SAW-rus).

But is it the *biggest*? Or were there even bigger dinosaurs roaming the earth millions of years ago? Absolutely. Their bones are still waiting for someone to find them!

5
Bones Tell Stories

Digging up dinosaurs can take months of hard work. Once out of the ground, the bones are shipped to museum laboratories. In the labs, scientists begin to work with the bones. And this work can take years.

First, the dinosaur fossils are unpacked. Plaster jackets are cut away. The thin wrapping is removed. Cracks in the bones are filled with glue. Any rock still attached to the bone is taken off with hand scrapers or dental drills.

Then geologists (jee-OL-uh-jists) study the rocks. They want to find out how old the rock is. So they test it for two things: potassium and argon. Over millions of years, potassium turns to argon. Geologists can tell a rock's age from the amount of potassium in it compared to the amount of argon. The more argon in a rock, the older it is.

The oldest dinosaur bones have been found in rocks 225 to 235 million years old. These dinosaurs were only about the size of a crocodile. Really giant dinosaurs did not show up until 190 to 144 million years ago. And in rocks from 144 to 65 million years ago, there are fossils from many, many dinosaurs of all shapes and sizes.

The rock surrounding a fossil can tell more than just a dinosaur's age. Are there plant fossils in the rock? They may be clues to what dinosaurs ate. Is the rock from a riverbed? This may be a clue to where dinosaurs lived.

Paleontologists also study the rocks. First, they look at photographs from the dig. The way bones are arranged in rock can tell a story.

Hundreds of skeletons of a small, bird-like dinosaur called *Coelophysis* (see-luh-FY-sis) were found together at a dig in New Mexico. This led paleontologists to think that *Coelophysis* traveled in packs. It also led them to think that these dinosaurs may have been caught in a flood and drowned.

Eventually, all the rock around the fossils is removed. Now paleontologists work on the fossils themselves. Sometimes they gather all the bones they think are from the same dinosaur. They lay them out on a huge, boxlike table. Then they try to put the bones together like a giant skeleton jigsaw puzzle.

Once the skeleton puzzle is put together, paleontologists look for clues. What do the bones tell about the dinosaur?

Are a dinosaur's front legs much shorter than its back legs? If so, it probably walked on its hind legs, like *Tyrannosaurus* (ty-RAN-uh-SAW-rus).

Are the leg bones thick and all about the same size? Then the dinosaur probably walked on all fours, like *Argentinosaurus*.

Paleontologists look for anything odd about the skeleton that could tell them about the dinosaur. The duck-billed *Corythosaurus* (kor-ITH-uh-SAW-rus) has a bony crest on its skull. The crest is connected to the dinosaur's nasal passage. The nasal passage is shaped sort of like a tuba or a trombone. So some paleontologists believe *Corythosaurus* could make trumpeting sounds. Each type of crested duck-billed dinosaur has a different shape nasal passage. This means each type would have made its own kind of "music"!

Finding new fossils can change what dinosaur hunters thought they knew about dinosaurs. For almost twenty years, *Majungatholus* (mah-JUNG-uh-THO-lus) was thought to be a plant-eater. Then dinosaur hunter Dr. Cathy Forster went on a dig in Madagascar. She and the rest of the crew dug up a *Majungatholus* skull. It was in excellent shape. It showed something no other skull had showed. This dinosaur had small, sharp teeth. This meant *Majungatholus* was really a meat-eater!

Paleontologists think that the bones of only one dinosaur out of every million that lived became fossils. But bones aren't the only storytellers. Fossilized dinosaur droppings, called coprolites (KOP-ruh-lites), can give clues to how dinosaurs lived. Dinosaur hunters found what they believe is a *Tyrannosaurus* dropping. It is nearly three feet long and weighs over twenty pounds. Inside the coprolite they found chewed-up bones from a plant-eater.

Fossil footprints can also show what certain dinosaurs were doing on a certain day millions of years ago. In Texas, some footprints of *Pleurocoelus* (PLOOR-uh-SEE-lus), a water-

loving plant-eater, were found in a riverbed. Nearby, the tracks of a fierce meat-eater, *Acrocanthosaurus* (ACK-ro-KAN-thuh-SAW-rus), appear in the mud. Was *Acrocanthosaurus* chasing *Pleurocoelus*? Nobody knows for sure, but it looks that way. The footprints go on. Suddenly, they stop. Did *Acrocanthosaurus* catch its prey? Or did *Pleurocoelus* escape? So far, no one has been able to tell.

Most fossils that are found belonged to adult dinosaurs. Their bones were big and heavy. Their teeth were large. They were more likely to become preserved as fossils than tiny bones or teeth, or delicate eggs.

But sometimes fossils of dinosaur eggs do turn up. The eggs of gigantic dinosaurs are about the size of cannonballs. When dinosaur babies hatched, they were smaller than human babies!

Most dinosaur hunters thought that dinosaurs left their eggs to hatch on their own, the way turtles and lizards do. But a group of fossilized dinosaur nests found in Montana show that this wasn't always true.

These mud nests were about seven feet across and three feet deep. They belonged to a kind of duck-billed dinosaur. Eggs were found in a few of the nests. One also had fifteen skeletons of dinosaur babies. Newly hatched babies of this type of dinosaur are about a foot long. But these babies were three feet long.